# With a

by Rowan Obach

illustrated by Tom McKee

**Scott Foresman**
is an imprint of

Glenview, Illinois • Boston, Massachusetts • Chandler, Arizona
Upper Saddle River, New Jersey

Every effort has been made to secure permission and provide appropriate credit for photographic material. The publisher deeply regrets any omission and pledges to correct errors called to its attention in subsequent editions.

Unless otherwise acknowledged, all photographs are the property of Scott Foresman, a division of Pearson Education.

Photo locators denoted as follows: Top (T), Center (C), Bottom (B), Left (L), Right (R), Background (Bkgd)

Illustrations by Tom McKee

Photograph 20 Brand X Pictures

ISBN 13: 978-0-328-51371-0
ISBN 10:    0-328-51371-7

**Copyright © by Pearson Education, Inc., or its affiliates. All rights reserved.**
Printed in the United States of America. This publication is protected by copyright, and permission should be obtained from the publisher prior to any prohibited reproduction, storage in a retrieval system, or transmission in any form or by any means, electronic, mechanical, photocopying, recording, or likewise. For information regarding permissions, write to Pearson Curriculum Rights & Permissions, One Lake Street, Upper Saddle River, New Jersey 07458.

**Pearson®** is a trademark, in the U.S. and/or in other countries, of Pearson plc or its affiliates.

**Scott Foresman®** is a trademark, in the U.S. and/or in other countries, of Pearson Education, Inc., or its affiliates.

10 11 12 13 V0FL 17 16 15 14

Jake heard the doorbell ring and jumped up to open the front door. His good friends Bo and Ruby were standing outside. "How's it going?" Jake asked, as he welcomed them into the house.

"We're looking for something fun to do," said Ruby. "And, we're hungry! Do you have anything to eat?"

"You two are always hungry," laughed Jake. "All right, let's find some food."

Ruby and Bo followed Jake into the kitchen, and Jake searched through the refrigerator. Finding some fresh pizza dough, he said, "Hey, I have an idea. Let's make a pizza . . . but with a twist."

"What do you mean?" Ruby asked. She looked confused.

"We have the dough," Jake explained, "but we don't have the other ingredients. Finding them will be the twist," he said with a wink.

"OK," said Bo. "Let's make a list, and then we can go shopping."

Jake, Bo, and Ruby started the list by writing down the basic ingredients for pizza—cheese, tomatoes, garlic.

"Write *basil* and *oregano* on the list too," Ruby told Jake.

"What?" asked Bo. "What are those?"

"They're seasonings," explained Jake. "They'll make the pizza taste great."

Jake, Bo, and Ruby finished off the list by adding *olives* and *pineapple*. Then they inspected their list until everyone was satisfied. Going shopping for the ingredients was the next step.

"Should we walk to the supermarket or ride our bikes?" asked Bo as they walked outside.

"I have a better idea," Jake replied, grinning mysteriously. "Get ready! Here comes the twist!" Jake snapped his fingers loudly, and suddenly everything was dark. The children felt like they were spinning through the air.

After a few seconds it was light again and they felt their feet back on the ground. When Jake, Bo, and Ruby looked around, they realized they were in a different place. The children were standing in a bustling outdoor market in the country of Peru!

"Wow!" said Bo. "This really is a twist!"

"This is incredible!" Ruby said, puzzled.

"Now you know my finger-snapping trick," said Jake. "This is where we'll get the tomatoes for our pizza!"

The market was set up along both sides of the road with awnings protecting the sellers and their products from the hot sun.

The vendors called out to Ruby, Jake, and Bo, showing off what they had to sell. There were sacks of flour, baskets of bread, and bunches of fresh flowers. Fruits and vegetables were stacked in neat piles. Ruby spotted the tomatoes and chose several ripe ones. She placed them in a string bag.

"Now we can cross tomatoes off the list," said Bo.

"That's right," agreed Jake. "Are we ready to move on?"

Bo and Ruby looked at each other nervously. "Oh boy," Ruby said. "I think Jake's going to do that thing with his fingers again. Get ready, Bo!"

Jake snapped his fingers again, and the children vanished from the market in Peru.

This time, Jake, Bo, and Ruby mysteriously appeared at an outdoor market in Italy. It was just after dawn in the town square, and the vendors were preparing to open the market. Young children were helping to hang cloths from wooden frames around each stand. The vendors placed their goods on the tables in the stands.

"Look," said Ruby. "We can buy shoes and sandals here."

"And there are radios for sale over here," called Bo, beckoning to the others.

"Come on, you two. We're here for the cheese, remember?" Jake reminded his excited friends.

Jake led Bo and Ruby to the food stands in one corner of the town square. There they saw salamis, sausages, fruits, vegetables, and cheeses. Jake looked at the shopping list and chose wedges of Parmesan and mozzarella. The vendor wrapped the cheeses in paper and Ruby placed the cheese bundles into the string bag, along with the tomatoes from Peru.

"That was a genuine Italian food market all right," said Jake. "Our pizza will be delicious with these wonderful cheeses. But we still have more shopping to do. Are you ready to travel again, my friends?"

By now, Bo and Ruby were getting used to Jake's finger snapping. "I'm really enjoying this shopping trip," Bo said, excitedly, as Jake snapped his fingers. In an instant, the children disappeared from the Italian food market.

Amazingly, Jake, Ruby, and Bo were transported to a bazaar in India. It was crowded with shoppers looking for bargains. Some local shoppers bought their food at nearby supermarkets, but most of the people in the village came to the bazaar for fruit, vegetables, fish, meat, and spices.

"Did you see the fruit stalls?" asked Ruby. "They've got oranges, bananas, mangoes, and papayas. All of this traveling is making me hungrier than ever!"

"Me too," said Bo. "Let's get what we need here, fast, so we can make that pizza!"

As Jake, Bo, and Ruby walked along, Jake pointed to one of the displays. "The basil is over there. That's one of the seasonings you asked about, Bo," Jake said to his friend.

The children made their way through the crowd to the basil vendor Jake had pointed out. They bought some basil and stored it in the string bag, along with the tomatoes from Peru and the cheeses from Italy.

Then Bo said, "Go ahead and snap your fingers, Jake. I'm starving!"

"Are you in a hurry, Bo?" Jake asked with a laugh. He snapped his fingers.

11

Within seconds, the three children were shivering on a chilly Russian street.

"I don't want to stay here in the cold too long," said Jake, his teeth chattering.

The children hurried toward the large covered market, where local people were selling their products. On their way they glanced at the outdoor stands, where books, clothes, shoes, and other goods were being sold. As cold as it was, there were many shoppers browsing among the items for sale.

Once inside the covered market, the three friends were amazed to see fresh vegetables piled high. "How could so many fresh vegetables be here in the middle of winter?" Ruby asked a vendor.

The vendor explained that the produce grew in nearby greenhouses. That way, people could enjoy fresh vegetables throughout the year.

"Then I bet you have fresh garlic here," said Jake. The vendor pointed the way to the garlic stand. The children bought a large garlic bulb. Into the string bag it went, along with the tomatoes from Peru, cheeses from Italy, and basil from India.

Jake snapped his fingers for the fifth time that day. Moments later, the children landed in a Greek market.

"Oh, smell the fish!" gasped Ruby as she held her nose. She laughed when Bo and Jake did the same.

The children wandered through the fish market and eventually found the spice vendors.

"Here's the oregano," Jake called out. He paid for some of the spice and crossed the word *oregano* off the list. Then he placed the oregano in the string bag.

Bo said, "Wow, look at all these vendors who sell olives. There must be a million different kinds!"

After finding some olives that looked good, Jake bought a whole carton and tossed it into the string bag. Looking at how the bag had expanded, he decided to check off the ingredients they had bought.

"OK, Ruby, I'll call off the ingredient, you make sure it's in the bag," Jake said.

"Right," Ruby replied.

"Tomatoes from Peru?" Jake asked.

"You bet," Ruby said.

"Cheeses from Italy?" Jake asked.

"Got 'em," Ruby said.

"Basil from India?" Jake asked.

"It's in the bag," Ruby said.

"Garlic from Russia?" Jake asked.

"A whole bulb," Ruby said.

"And oregano and olives from Greece?" Jake asked.

"We're all set," Ruby said.

"Great, then we're off!" Jake said, and he snapped his fingers.

"This is our last stop," said Jake as the three children arrived at a Brazilian *feira*, or street market. The weekly market was overflowing with exotic fruits and vegetables.

Ruby picked up a tiny bunch of bananas. "I know what these are, of course," she said. "But what is that?" she asked as she pointed to another fruit.

"It's persimmon," said the vendor. He offered some cut-up pieces to the children.

"Delicious!" said Bo. "Do you know where we can find some pineapple?"

The vendor pointed to an area where pineapple was sold. The three children went over to the pineapple stand and bought a whole one. Ruby stowed the pineapple in the string bag along with the other ingredients. Then Jake held up the shopping list and saw every item had been crossed off the list!

Bo let out a cheer. "It's time to make the pizza!" he said. "Take us home, Jake."

With two quick snaps of his fingers, Jake brought them all back to his house.

Jake, Ruby, and Bo stood in Jake's kitchen. Ruby was clutching the string bag full of ingredients.

The children quickly divided up the tasks for making the pizza. Jake prepared the pizza dough in the pan. He unwrapped the cheeses and grated the Parmesan and sliced the mozzarella. Ruby mashed the tomatoes with the basil, oregano, and garlic. Then she put them into the pot to cook. Bo carefully sliced the olives and the pineapple.

When the sauce was cooked, Jake's mom came in from her study to spoon it onto the pizza dough. After that Jake layered the mozzarella on the sauce and sprinkled the Parmesan on top. Finally, Bo carefully arranged the olives and pineapple in patterns on top of the cheeses. Mom then helped place the pizza in the hot oven for the children.

"How did you come up with such wonderful ingredients for this pizza?" Mom asked the children.

"Oh, we have our ways," Jake said, winking at Bo and Ruby.

Soon the pizza was ready. Jake asked Mom to take it out of the oven for them. The hungry children ate the whole pizza, right down to the last crumb.

"Thanks, Jake!" said Bo and Ruby.

"That's pizza . . . with a twist!" said Jake with a big smile.

# The History of Pizza

Pizza became popular in Naples, Italy, in the late 1700s. Then, in 1889, news of the local dish began to spread when Queen Margherita and King Umberto I visited Naples.

For that special occasion, Naples' most famous pizza chef prepared a new kind of pizza for the king and queen. He used tomato sauce, mozzarella cheese, and basil leaves. The red tomato sauce, white mozzarella, and green basil were specially chosen to match the red, white, and green of the Italian flag. The queen liked the pizza so much that it was named pizza Margherita in her honor.

Today, there are many restaurants in the United States where you can order pizza Margherita. And, of course, you can make your own!